## TEACHERS' HOLIDAY HELPERS

# Valentine's Day
## Activities for the Primary Grades

by Judy Beach and Kathleen Spencer

**Fearon Teacher Aids**
a division of
**David S. Lake Publishers**
Belmont, California

ISBN 0-8224-6774-7

Printed in the United States of America

1. 9 8 7 6 5

# Contents

## Teacher Guide

## Activity Sheets

# Teacher Guide

## Introduction

*Teachers' Holiday Helpers* provides busy teachers with high-quality, easy-to-prepare lessons for the primary classroom. The charming characters on the activity pages and the easy-to-make bulletin board display generate anticipation for the events of Valentine's Day.

In this book you will find everything you need to provide practice in essential skills and to develop students' enthusiasm for Valentine's Day. A bulletin board design, patterns, and instructions are given for instant bulletin board success. You can follow the instructions to prepare a duplicate of the sample design, or you can reproduce the patterns and create your own design. In combination with the children's activity sheets from this book, or as a separate decorative display, the bulletin board is sure to be a hit in your classroom.

The first two activities are designed to develop your students' interest in the coming of Valentine's Day. You may want to begin by using the calendar to show students when to expect Valentine's Day. The next activity, dramatizing a finger play, will develop the students' listening and language skills and will introduce them to the characters that appear on the activity pages.

There are twenty additional activity sheets to help you develop students' skills in reading, math, creative writing, and art. Each reproducible worksheet is accented with delightful Valentine's Day characters for your students to color.

The final two activities are open worksheets that are designed for flexibility in planning additional practice in addition and subtraction. Write your choice of math problems in the work spaces and the answers at the bottom of the pages. Students can then add, subtract, cut and paste, or cross off the answers as directed.

# Bulletin Board Display

You may copy or enlarge the Valentine's Day bulletin board patterns according to the proportions that are determined by the size of your bulletin board space. You may wish to make more than one tracing of the patterns in different sizes for use in several places in your classroom. Tracings can be made by using either an opaque or overhead projector. You can trace the images onto a white surface and then color them using crayons, pastels, or paints. Or you might trace selected parts of the characters (hair, eyes, clothing) onto sheets of colored construction paper and overlay them on the final images.

To make a tracing using an opaque projector, simply place the pattern in the projector and focus the projection on a sheet of paper or tagboard that is sized according to your needs. Then trace the image. To make a tracing using an overhead projector, make a transparency of the pattern and place the transparency on the projector. Focus the image and trace it onto your paper or tagboard.

**Basic Steps**
To make the bulletin board display that is shown above, follow these simple steps:
1. Reproduce the bulletin board patterns in this book. Adjust their sizes to the area of your bulletin board. (If you want to add different textures to the characters, see the section "Extra Textures.")

2. Cover the bulletin board with light blue paper.
3. Staple or pin the separate pieces into place.

**Extra Textures**

**balloons:** Use sheets of tissue paper for the balloons. Attach colorful yarn for the strings. Make the bow from brightly colored ribbon.

**bear:** Trace the bear onto felt or fuzzy paper. Use a yarn pompon for the nose.

**penguin:** Put a cloth scarf around the penguin's neck.

**snail:** Use pipe cleaners to make the antennae.

**dog:** Trace the dog onto felt or fuzzy paper. Attach a yarn pompon for the nose. Use a real dog collar, or make the dog's collar from a piece of colorful ribbon. Decorate the ribbon with sequins, beads, or glitter.

Be Mine

I Love You

Teachers' Holiday Helpers ● *Valentine's Day,* © 1987 David S. Lake Publishers

**Valentine's Day**

Be My Valentine

Happy Valentine's Day

# Calendar and Finger Play Guide

### February calendar, page 8

The calendar may be completed to help orient the children to the events of February. Reproduce enough calendars to provide one for each child and one for demonstration. Show the children how to write the name of the month and where to write the numbers that represent the dates. Discuss the date of Valentine's Day with respect to other events in February, for example, school holidays and children's birthdays. Children will learn from this orientation, and their anticipation will increase as you use the other Valentine-theme activities in this book.

### Dramatization with finger puppets, page 9

Plan to provide each child with two or three finger puppets (one or two character puppets and one blank heart puppet as the Valentine for their secret friend). Reproduce the patterns onto heavy paper or lightweight cardboard. You may want to cut the puppets apart before distributing them to the children. Have the children color and cut out their puppets. They can then tape the puppets to straws.

Discuss several aspects of finger puppetry: listening, moving puppets at appropriate times, speaking clearly, and so on. Read the poem to the children. Discuss the characters and their actions. Discuss the ways the children might move their puppets. Allow the children to practice reciting each stanza of the poem and moving or resting their puppets appropriately before they dramatize the entire poem.

### A Valentine's Day Poem

Friends are very special
That's why I chose today,
To send each one a Valentine
That I made a special way.

The first one went to a puppy
Who doesn't have a name,
I only got her yesterday
But I love her just the same.

The second one went to a bunny
Who lives inside his hutch,
I feed him all the vegetables
That my mom gives me for lunch.

The third one went to a panda
Who promised me to keep,
All the secrets that we'd shared
Before we fell asleep.

The fourth one went to a turtle
Who lives inside her shell,
I'd like to take her for a walk,
But she doesn't move too well.

The fifth one went to someone
That only I can tell,
We play together all day long;
We know each other well.

Name _____

Be Mine

*Teachers' Holiday Helpers • Valentine's Day,* © 1987 David S. Lake Publishers

| Sunday | Monday | Tuesday | Wednesday | Thursday | Friday | Saturday |
|--------|--------|---------|-----------|----------|--------|----------|
|        |        |         |           |          |        |          |
|        |        |         |           |          |        |          |
|        |        |         |           |          |        |          |
|        |        |         |           |          |        |          |
|        |        |         |           |          |        |          |

8 • Completing a calendar                                      **Valentine's Day**

**To the teacher:**

Reproduce the activity sheet on page 11. Each student will need an activity sheet and a set of crayons in the eight basic colors. Read the directions on this sheet to your students.

**Say:**

Lester Lion delivers the mail to all his friends in the woods. His friends are Carmine Cat, Biffy Bear, and Daphine Duck. Listen and follow these directions as I read them aloud to you.

Start at Lester Lion.
1. Find the hearts in Lester's bag. Color them yellow.
2. Draw one blue button on Lester's jacket.
3. Lester needs a tail. Draw one long brown tail on Lester.
4. Find the path that leads to Carmine Cat. Draw four purple footprints on the path.

Look at Carmine Cat.
1. Draw a black fishing pole in Carmine's paw.
2. Draw two small orange fish in the water.
3. Color the water around the fish blue.
4. Lester gave Carmine a yellow heart. Draw it on the tree stump.
5. Find the path to Biffy Bear. Put six red footprints on the path.

Look at Biffy Bear.
1. Draw another black and yellow bee next to Biffy.
2. Biffy is standing on some blades of grass. Draw seven blades of grass under Biffy's feet.
3. Color Biffy brown.
4. Lester left a yellow heart for Biffy. Draw it on the beehive.
5. Find the path leading to Daphine Duck. Put two brown footprints on the path.

Look at Daphine Duck.
1. Put a big yellow sun in the sky above Daphine.
2. Daphine needs feet. Draw two orange circles for her feet.
3. Draw a small yellow triangle for Daphine's wing.
4. Lester left one yellow heart for Daphine. Draw it on her head.

Name _____

Name _____

Cut out and then paste the pictures to make pairs of rhyming words.

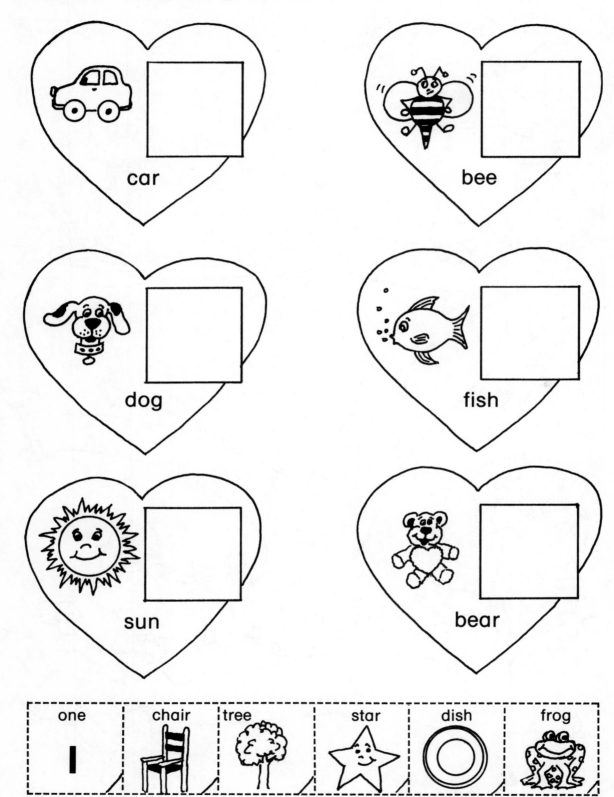

car

bee

dog

fish

sun

bear

| one | chair | tree | star | dish | frog |

Teachers' Holiday Helpers • Valentine's Day, © 1987 David S. Lake Publishers

**Valentine's Day**

Name _____

 Use the key. Color the hearts.

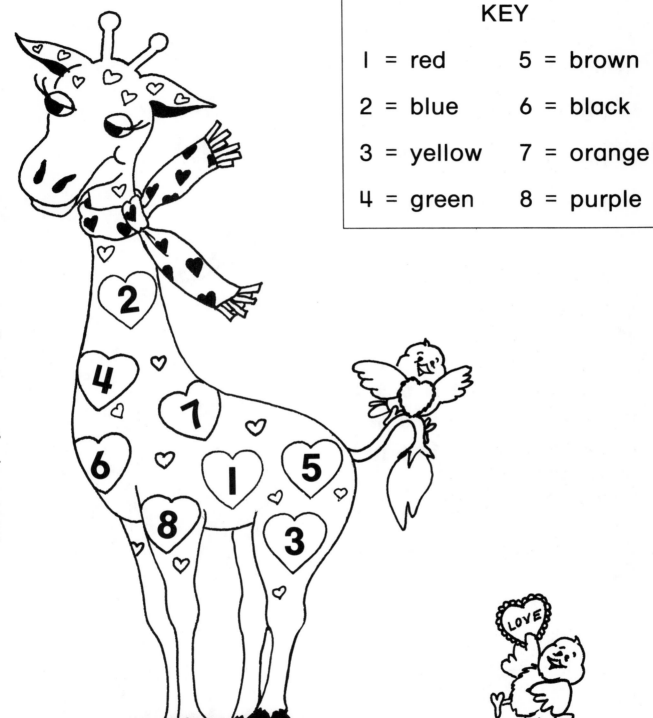

KEY

1 = red      5 = brown

2 = blue     6 = black

3 = yellow   7 = orange

4 = green    8 = purple

Name _____

Find the hidden words. Circle the words in the heart as you find them.

friends

flowers

happy

heart

love

treat

```
c o f r i e n d s b
k a b o l o v e w y
h e a r t o f o m t
r e s f l o w e r s
d f k x r h a p p y
g o t r e a t o n a
```

*Teachers' Holiday Helpers • Valentine's Day,* © 1987 David S. Lake Publishers

Name _____

Write a Valentine's Day message. Use some of the words below.

be mine

happy

heart

love

please

Name _____

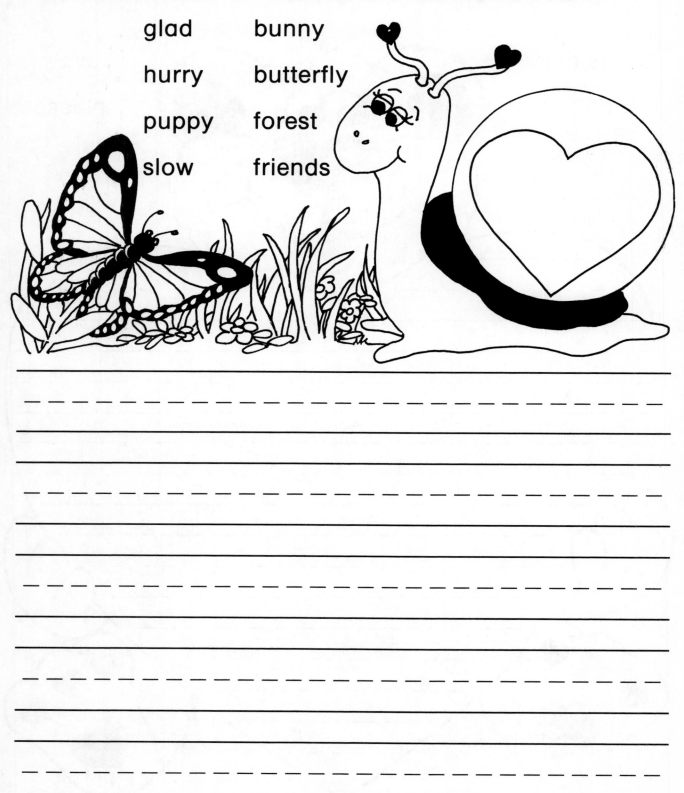

Write a story. Tell how the snail gave out her valentine cards. Use some of the words below.

glad     bunny

hurry     butterfly

puppy     forest

slow     friends

Teachers' Holiday Helpers • Valentine's Day, © 1987 David S. Lake Publishers

Name _____

Cut out and then paste the squares and rectangles to complete the picture.

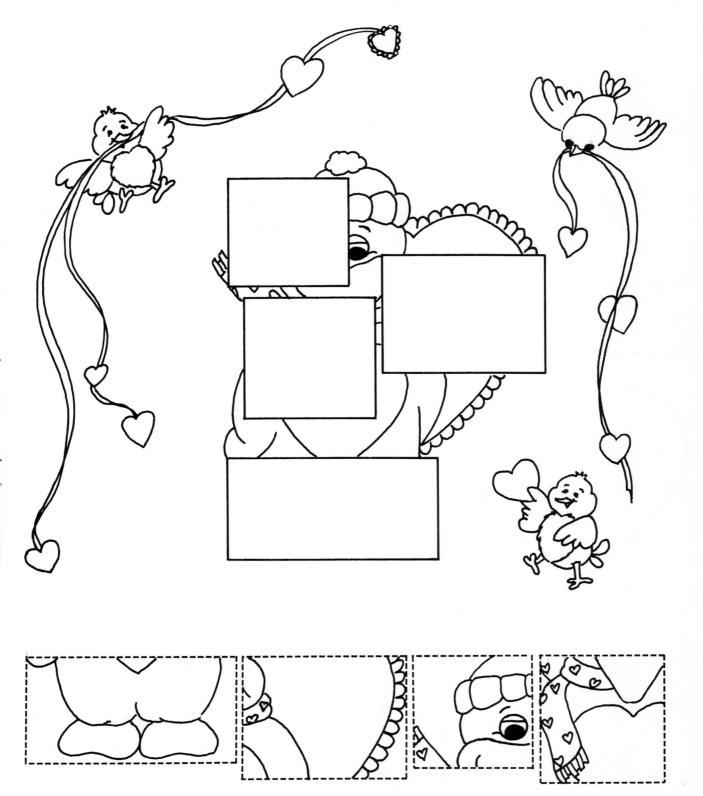

Name _____

To make the valentine bird, do this:
Color the parts. Cut out the parts.

Paste the  ▽  on the  .
Paste the  ♡♡  on the .

paste here

paste
here

paste
here

Name _____

For each set of boxes, write the numbers in correct counting order.

8, 11, 9, 10

12, 15, 13, 14

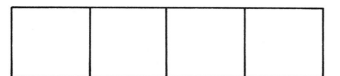

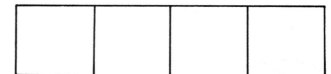

6, 9, 8, 7

13, 10, 12, 11

Name _____

Draw lines to connect the number words in counting order. Start with **one.** When you are finished, color the picture.

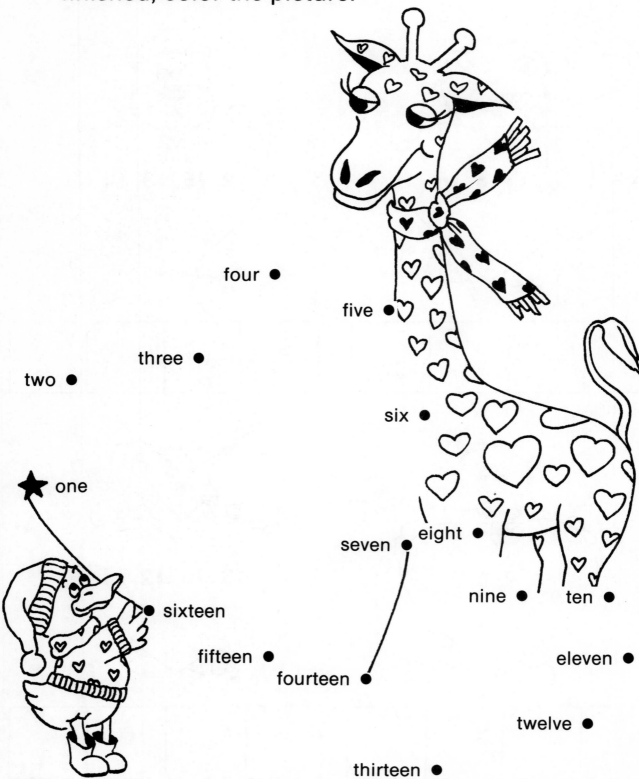

four •

five •

three •

two •

six •

one

seven •    eight •

nine •    ten •

sixteen •

eleven •

fifteen •

fourteen •

twelve •

thirteen •

*Teachers' Holiday Helpers • Valentine's Day,* © 1987 David S. Lake Publishers

**Valentine's Day**

Name _____

For each big heart, count the little hearts. In the boxes, write the numbers that tell how many.

**Add the numbers. Color each answer apple as you use it.**

|     |     |     |     |     |
|-----|-----|-----|-----|-----|
| 4<br>+ 5 | 2<br>+ 8 | 8<br>+ 5 | 6<br>+ 5 | 7<br>+ 7 |
| ☐ | ☐ | ☐ | ☐ | ☐ |

|     |     |     |     |     |
|-----|-----|-----|-----|-----|
| 6<br>+ 2 | 5<br>+ 7 | 8<br>+ 9 | 9<br>+ 7 | 6<br>+ 9 |
| ☐ | ☐ | ☐ | ☐ | ☐ |

8  9  10  11  12

13  14  15  16  17

*Teachers' Holiday Helpers • Valentine's Day,* © 1987 David S. Lake Publishers

Name _____

 Add the numbers. Color each answer heart as you use it.

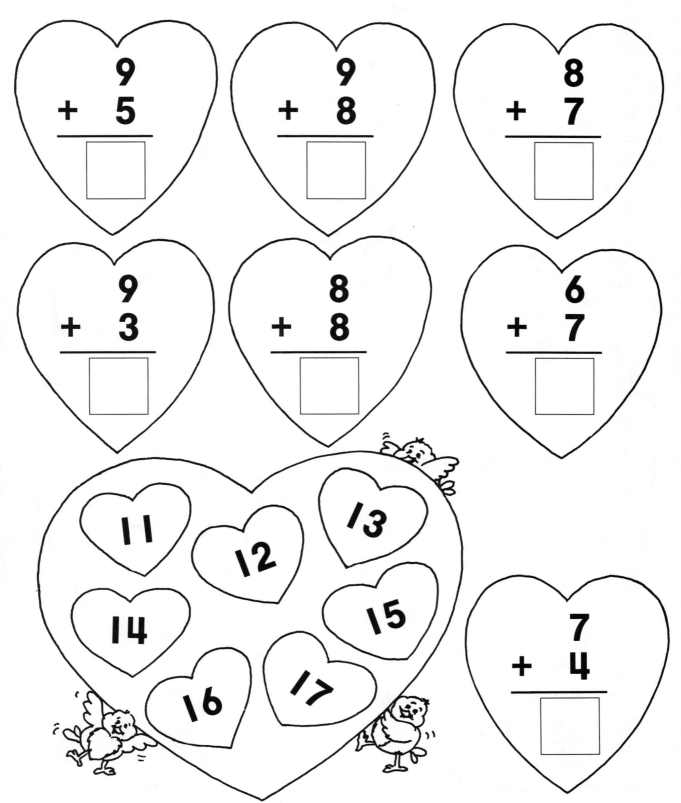

9 + 5

9 + 8

8 + 7

9 + 3

8 + 8

6 + 7

11  12  13

14  15

16  17

7 + 4

*Teachers' Holiday Helpers • Valentine's Day,* © 1987 David S. Lake Publishers

Name _____

Subtract the numbers and write the answers.
Use the key and color the bones.

KEY

2 = yellow
3 = purple
4 = orange
5 = green
6 = blue
7 = brown
8 = red

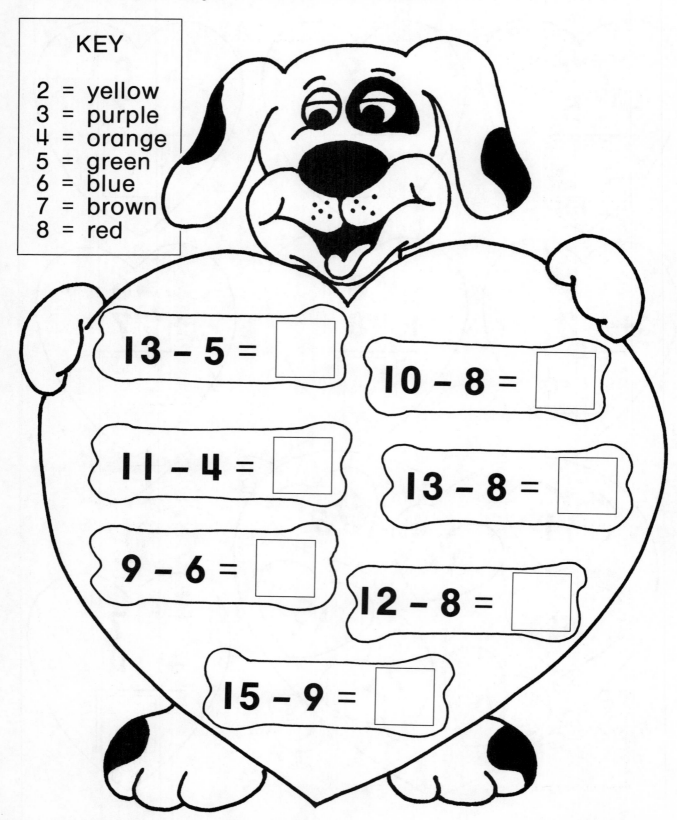

13 – 5 = 

10 – 8 = 

11 – 4 = 

13 – 8 = 

9 – 6 = 

12 – 8 = 

15 – 9 = 

Teachers' Holiday Helpers • Valentine's Day, © 1987 David S. Lake Publishers

**Valentine's Day**

Subtract the numbers. Write the answers.

Color the 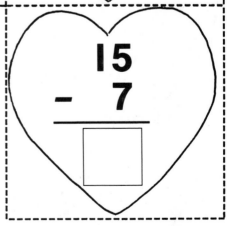 .

Cut on all the dotted lines. Use the parts on the next page.

$$14 - 6 = \boxed{\phantom{0}}$$

$$16 - 7 = \boxed{\phantom{0}}$$

$$17 - 9 = \boxed{\phantom{0}}$$

$$15 - 6 = \boxed{\phantom{0}}$$

$$16 - 9 = \boxed{\phantom{0}}$$

$$14 - 7 = \boxed{\phantom{0}}$$

$$15 - 7 = \boxed{\phantom{0}}$$

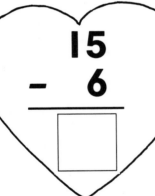

Teachers' Holiday Helpers • Valentine's Day, © 1987 David S. Lake Publishers

Name _____

 Use the parts from the subtraction page. Do this:
Color the picture.

Paste the  on the [picture] .

Put the hearts in the pocket.

paste here

paste here

paste here

Teachers' Holiday Helpers • Valentine's Day, © 1987 David S. Lake Publishers

Name _____

Solve the problems. Cut out and then paste the correct answers to complete each heart.

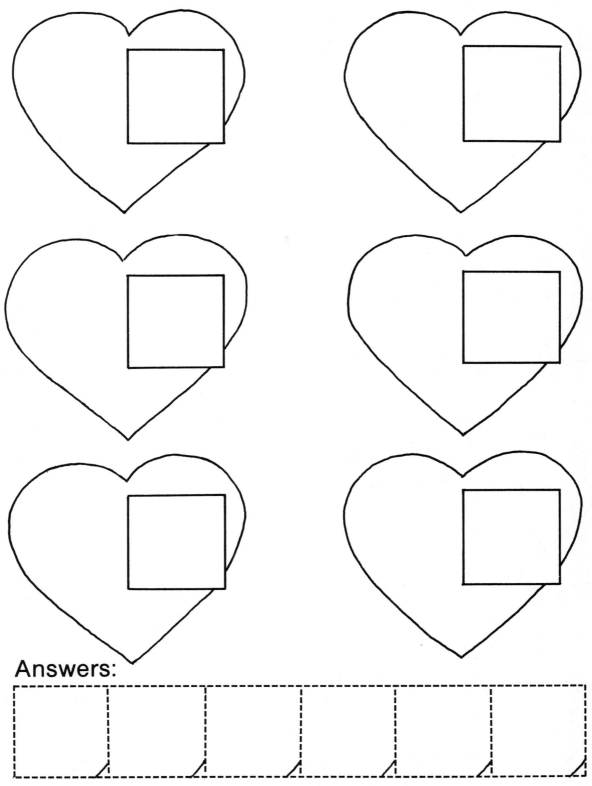

Answers:

Name _____

Solve the problems. As you use each answer, cross it off the big answer heart below.

Answers:

Teachers' Holiday Helpers • *Valentine's Day*, © 1987 David S. Lake Publishers

**Valentine's Day**